THE GREAT BALLOON PARTY BOOK

The Do-It-Yourself Guide to Throwing Your Own Fantastic Balloon-Theme Party

AARON FLANDERS

Contemporary Books

Chicago   New York   San Francisco   Lisbon   London   Madrid   Mexico City
Milan   New Delhi   San Juan   Seoul   Singapore   Sydney   Toronto

Library of Congress Cataloging-in-Publication Data

Flanders, Aaron.
    The great balloon party book : the do-it-yourself guide to throwing your own fantastic balloon-theme party / Aaron Flanders.
      p.   cm.
    ISBN 0-07-143746-0
    1. Balloon sculpture.   2. Games.   I. Title.

TT926.H784   2003
745.594—dc22   2003059165

1 2 3 4 5 6 7 8 9 0   KGP/KGP   2 1 0 9 8 7 6 5 4 3

ISBN 0-07-143746-0

Interior photos by David Caras
Interior design by Steve Straus

McGraw-Hill books are available at special quantity discounts to use as premiums and sales promotions, or for use in corporate training programs. For more information, please write to the Director of Special Sales, Professional Publishing, McGraw-Hill, Two Penn Plaza, New York, NY 10121-2298. Or contact your local bookstore.

This book is printed on acid-free paper.

Contents

CHAPTER 1

A Balloon Menagerie: Teaching a Group of People How to Make a Balloon Critter 1

CHAPTER 2

Fun, Fantastical Balloon Party Games 121

Acknowledgments

I'd like to thank my children, Adriel and Raphaela, who have been the most amazing participants and the most eager and willing audience that I could ever imagine. Their pure exuberance, joy, and moments of spontaneous happiness, with and without balloons, have been great and constant rewards for me.

I'd also like to thank my enthusiastic editor, Denise Betts, for her ever-present humor and encouragement; my publisher, Philip Ruppel, for immediately thinking this was a good idea and then helping to make it happen; and everyone at Contemporary Books/McGraw-Hill who had a finger in this project.

My marvelously gleeful and adorably energetic balloon-game models are Adriel Hsu-Flanders, Raphaela Hsu-Flanders, Alex Stange, Madelyn Herzog, Norah Herzog, Julian Bercu, Toby Bercu, Chiara Bercu, Natalia Forbath, and Sasha Forbath. Thanks for showing me that these games are actually thrilling and fun.

Introduction

Welcome to the wonderful, wacky world of balloons! Balloons of all shapes, sizes, and colors are a fantastically fun staple at any party or festive gathering. In this book, you'll learn how to highlight your party with balloon-animal-making activities and rip-roaring balloon games for all ages. The photos throughout will help you teach your party participants how to twist, squish, and pull pencil balloons into a variety of animal shapes, characters, and even hats to dress up any occasion. In addition, you'll discover hilarious and high-spirited balloon games you can play indoors or outdoors using round balloons. Think of it as your complete balloon party all in one convenient place. All you need to do is provide the guests, some cupcakes, and a good attitude and let this book be your guide to fun-filled balloon activities. Sit back, relax, and flip through this book to find an animal or two to practice making before the party. That way, you'll be a seasoned pro when you teach the other party participants how to make their own shapes. Imagine how proud you'll be when you hear your guests oohing and aahing over your professional-looking purple balloon pooch.

Remember, there's nothing difficult or tricky about making balloon animals. The rubber balloons used for these creations are strong and sturdy and survive a great deal of twisting and turning. Keep this in mind when you're making your balloon mouse, whose tiny twists scare even the most seasoned sculptor in anticipation of hearing a loud pop. I'll give you some tips a bit later in the book for ensuring the long life of your pencil balloons, but for now, just know that you shouldn't fear the balloons; they are your friend.

Although completed balloon shapes look impressive and magical, and children and adults alike marvel over how they are created seemingly out of thin air from a long, tubular piece of rubber, balloon animals are fairly easy to make. There's no trickery involved, and there are no special secrets passed from generation to generation of magicians and clowns. By carefully reading the instructions and patiently executing them, anyone and everyone—and that means you!—will be able to teach a group of friends and relatives, no matter how goofy, how to make some pretty cool balloon animals. All that, and you'll soon be a hero in your guests' eyes.

The Colorful History of Balloons

Balloons have been used to bring cheer and joy to children and adults for decades. No children's party is complete without a bunch of festively colored round balloons. Even trips to the dentist, which are no fun for adults either, are endured by anxious kids who are often rewarded for their bravery with the balloon of their choice. Balloons herald the grand openings of stores, political events, and school classrooms to rouse children and adults alike and get them excited about the event. Entertainers on the street and at circuses and parties sculpt balloons into amazingly lifelike shapes for people of all ages.

While no one knows the exact date, balloon animals probably made their first appearance in the United States (and most likely the world) sometime during the early 1960s. Around this time, Magic, Inc., now a famous magic store in Chicago, published a small booklet by a Chicagoan named Jimmy Davis that explained and illustrated how to make 15 different balloon animals using a single balloon. Soon after, several other booklets appeared, but none was widely circulated, and certainly average joes like you and me couldn't get their hands on them. Instead, these booklets were written for and sold to professional performers, including magicians, clowns, mimes, and the like. For many years creating balloon animals remained a rather obscure art form left mostly in the nimble hands of these entertainers.

At long last, in 1988 my first book, *Balloon Animals* (Contemporary Books), was published. The first of its kind to address an audience of nonperformers, the book came packaged with a variety of multicolored balloons and a hand pump to make them easier to inflate. The popularity of that book showed that anyone can make balloon animals and that a lot of people want to. The process of sculpting balloon animals was demystified.

In the years since, the act of sculpting balloons into various shapes and forms has exploded into a thriving art form. Well-known balloon sculptors such as Marvin Hardy, Royal Sorell, Todd Neufeld, and Larry Moss, to name but a few, have created balloon animals and sculptures that you wouldn't believe were possible, and thousands of people attend dramatic balloon-sculpture competitions around the world.

Balloon games have been around for as long as anyone ever had the idea to fill an "airship" (basically anything that will hold air—in the old days that could have been a stitched leather bag, a pig's bladder, or the skin of any animal) and play around with it. Latex balloons didn't hit the scene until 1918. Today, round balloons are ubiquitous, found in virtually every supermarket, toy store, and drugstore and at virtually every party (including yours!) in the world.

And now, to reward you for having survived this history lesson, let's get on with the show and learn how to teach your friends and family how to make their own balloon critters.

CHAPTER 1

A Balloon Menagerie

Teaching a Group of People How to Make a Balloon Critter

Having a group of people fashion animals out of brightly colored balloons can become an incredibly cool, highly interactive, loud, squeaky, hands-on event—truly fun for all ages. During these activities your friends and family will produce a variety of intriguing shapes (what was that supposed to be?) and will probably have animated discussions over the three-legged dogs and misshapen mice they'll end up with.

In this book, you'll find instructions for 10 different balloon animals. Read through all of them and pick one that strikes your fancy. Seven of them are for complete beginners, and three of them are slightly more advanced (intermediate) for people who might have done this before. The instructions are detailed and simple enough so that even the intermediate animals are appropriate for beginners with a little bit of patience and dexterous fingers. All of the animals are fun to make and will provide a highly charged creative experience at any party. So, without further ado, here are the steps to take to set up your balloon-animal-making party:

1. Pick someone who is willing to lead the activity. This person doesn't have to have any prior experience with balloon animals, but it will help if he or she is comfortable speaking in front of a crowd and demonstrating an activity. Let's assume this person is you.

2. Inflate and tie a balloon for each person who is participating. Be sure to pay careful attention to the amount of air and, more specifically, to the amount of uninflated tail to be left in each balloon. Each animal requires a different amount of uninflated tail to be left at the end, and it's crucial that this measurement be pretty close to the instructions to allow for the different twists required of each particular animal.

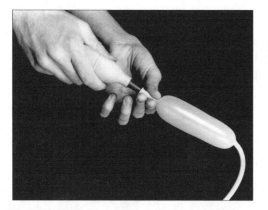

Inflating the Balloon

1. Stretch the balloon a few times before you inflate it. Slip the end of the balloon over the nozzle of the pump. Roll the neck of the balloon onto the nozzle about one inch. Hold it in place with the thumb and index finger of one hand. With your other hand, slowly begin inflating the balloon by squeezing and releasing the bulb of the pump.

2. Fill the balloon until you have the desired amount of uninflated balloon at the end (the tail). This tail will allow you to make many twists in the balloon. It allows the air in the balloon to expand as you make your twists.

3. Slip the neck of the balloon off the nozzle of the pump, but continue pinching the neck of the balloon to keep the air inside.

Tying the Balloon

1. Let a tiny bit of air out of the balloon so that the neck of the balloon is a little longer and more flexible. Hold the neck of the balloon between your thumb and index finger.

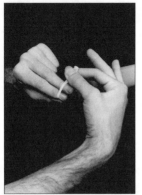

2. Stretch the neck of the balloon over the backs of your index and middle fingers.

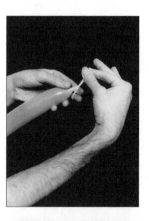

3. Continue stretching the neck of the balloon around the fronts of your index and middle fingers.

4. If you separate your index and middle fingers, you will create a small space.

5. Push the neck of the balloon through this space.

6. Holding the neck of the balloon, slide the rest of the balloon off your index and middle fingers.

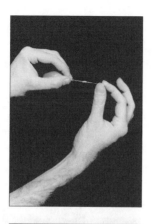

7. Give a little tug, and you have your knot.

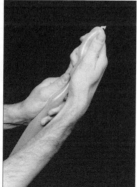

8. Squeeze each balloon gently at the knot end to lessen the tension of the balloon behind the knot.

When the Balloon Is Inflated

No matter how tempted you are, don't run your hands up and down the sides of the balloon, and be sure to discourage your guests from doing so. Besides making an uncomfortably irritating and loud squeaking noise, this will weaken the sides of the balloon and could cause it to pop. Naturally, you should keep your inflated balloon away from any sharp objects, including the floor, which always has tiny little sharp things that you can't see but that could pop your balloon.

Before You Start

The first thing you want to emphasize to everyone at the party is that there is nothing difficult about making balloon animals. In fact, it's so easy, anyone can do it! The balloons are designed to be pulled and pinched and twisted, and they are extra strong to allow for plenty of manipulation. Also, your hands have performed far more complicated activities than what you are about to do, including writing really tiny letters with a small pencil or threading a needle. Occasionally a balloon will pop, but it won't hurt you, and the noise, while surprising, isn't a huge explosion. The squeaking noise made by the twisting and turning of the balloons might bother some people, but they'll soon get used to the sound and even forget about it as they concentrate on making their own animal.

It's generally a lot easier for a group of people to learn how to make balloon animals if the leader first demonstrates each of the moves for the group before everyone tries them on their own balloon. For this reason, you should review the instructions for making the balloon animals and do a trial run before leading any of the activities. This will give you a little bit of practice and will make for a more polished group twisting session. Now it's time to jump right in and make your first animal: man's best friend, the balloon dog.

Man's Best Friend: The Balloon Dog

(BEGINNER'S LEVEL)

The balloon dog is the perfect critter to make for people who are doing this for the very first time. It's super easy, very cute, and requires three "twisting-and-locking" maneuvers that are essential to most balloon animals. No two balloon dogs ever look exactly alike, so each person will feel as if they've created their own one-of-a-kind breed.

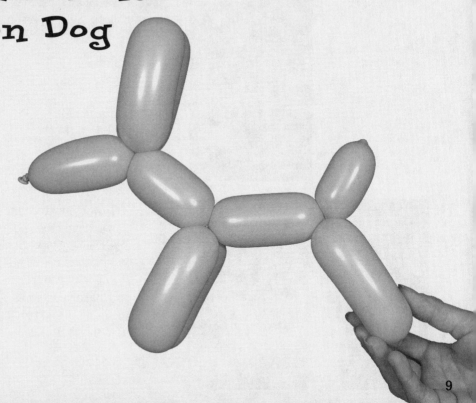

1. Pass out an inflated balloon with a three-inch tail of uninflated balloon to each person who would like to participate.

2. Ask everyone to find the end of the balloon that has the knot in it and hold the knot end of the balloon up in front of them. You will begin twisting the balloon from the end that has the knot and twist toward the end that has the tail. This will allow the air in the balloon to move downward toward the tail as you make your twists. Ask everyone to pinch the balloon with their thumb and index finger of one hand, about three inches from the knot. Demonstrate for everyone first.

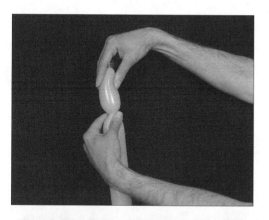

3. Ask everyone to take their free hand and twist this three-inch section of balloon around, two full turns, away from their body. This twist forms the nose of their dog. Demonstrate this for everyone before they try it on their own balloon.

4. Tell everyone that they must hold onto this twist gently with the thumb and index finger of one hand to prevent it from untwisting. Make sure you pause and hold up your balloon to demonstrate.

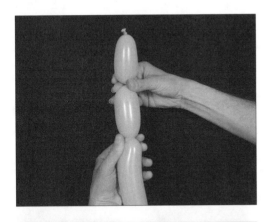

5. Ask everyone to hold onto their first twist so that it doesn't untwist and to pinch their balloon three inches below that first three-inch bubble. Ask them to twist both their hands in opposite directions until their balloon twists again at the point that they are pinching. This second bubble will form one of the ears of their balloon dog. Again, demonstrate this move for everyone before they try it themselves.

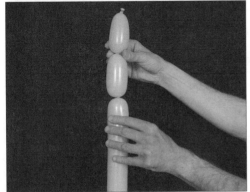

6. Tell everyone that they must continue holding onto both twists so that they don't untwist. Demonstrate.

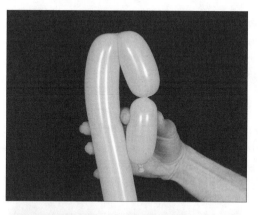

7. Ask everyone to fold the two bubbles that they have just created down alongside the length of the balloon. Demonstrate.

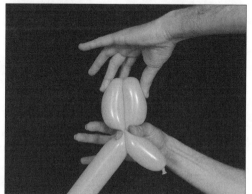

8. Show everyone how to pinch their length of balloon at the point where it meets their first twist. This will form the second ear of their dog. Ask everyone to watch this next move closely, before they try it on their own balloon. Twist both of the ears by rotating them together, about two full turns around. Demonstrate slowly, and untwist and repeat this move if people ask to see it again.

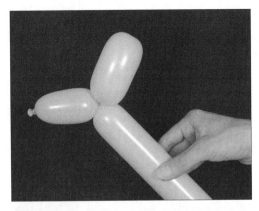

9. This third twist will lock the first two twists of everyone's animal, and it allows everyone to let go of the nose-and-ears section of their dog. This twist is referred to as a *locking twist*. Everyone's hands are now free to finish the rest of their dog. The three twists that you've just learned in making your balloon dog are the only three twists that you need to know to complete your balloon dog. Everyone will now repeat those three twists, in their entirety, two more times, and their balloon dog will be finished. Be sure to have everyone hold up their nose-and-ears section at this point so everyone can look around at each other's creations.

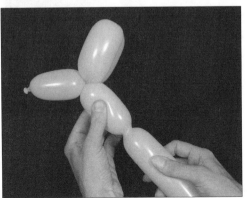

10. With everyone's nose-and-ears section of their dog finished and locked into place with a locking twist, have everyone pinch their balloon, with their thumb and index finger of one hand, about three inches below their nose-and-ears section. Holding one hand above and one hand below this point on their balloon, have everyone turn both their hands in opposite directions until their balloon twists at that point. This bubble will be the neck of their balloon dog.

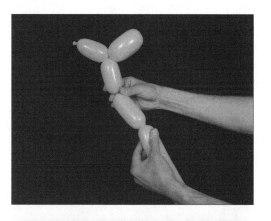

11. Show everyone again how to hold this twist gently with the thumb and index finger of one of their hands. While everyone is holding that twist, have them measure another three inches below that twist, just as they did before. Have them turn both their hands in opposite directions above and below this point, until the balloon twists again (at least two full turns). Remember to tell everyone that they have to hold onto both of these twists for just a couple more minutes until they make a locking twist. This second bubble will be one of their dog's front legs.

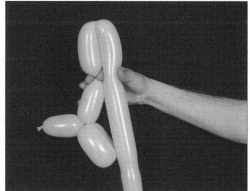

12. Have everyone fold these two bubbles down alongside their remaining length of balloon. Have them pinch their remaining length of balloon at the point where it meets the first twist. The two bubbles formed by their pinch will be the two front legs of their dog.

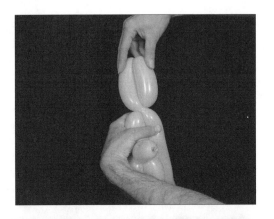

13. Have everyone twist both of the front legs around, using a locking twist, two full turns. This will lock all three of their twists and will free their hands to finish the rest of their dog. Everyone now has the nose, ears, neck, and front legs of their dog.

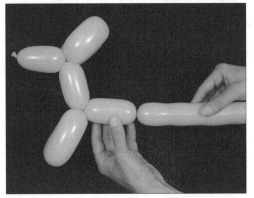

14. Have everyone pinch off another three-inch bubble beneath the neck-and-front-legs section of their dog. Have them twist the balloon again at this point; by now they're pretty familiar with that move. Make sure everyone remembers to hold onto the twist gently to prevent it from untwisting. This will be the body section of everyone's dog.

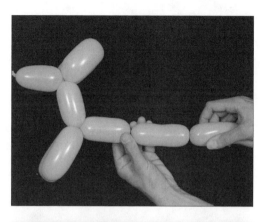

15. While everyone is gently holding that twist, have them all pinch off another three-inch bubble beneath the one that they have just made. Have them all make a twist in the balloon at this point. This second bubble will form one of their dog's back legs. Make sure everyone remembers to keep holding onto both twists.

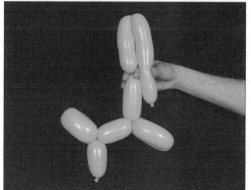

16. Have everyone fold these two bubbles down alongside the remaining length of balloon. Then have everyone pinch the last length of the balloon at the point where it meets the first twist. This bubble will form the other back leg of everyone's dog.

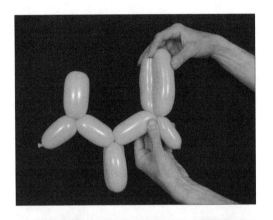

17. Have everyone use a locking twist and twist both of the back legs around two full turns. This locks the body-and-back-legs section. Be sure that everyone leaves a little bubble at the very end for their dog's tail.

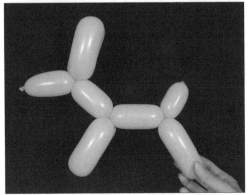

18. Have everyone play with the different parts of their balloon dog (gently) until it looks somewhat like the dog in the photo. Don't worry if your proportions are a little off; everyone will get better with practice. And I've never seen a balloon dog that I didn't like. Have everyone hold their balloon dog up so that each person can see all the different kinds of dogs that everyone made. Congratulations! You've just taught your first balloon-animal workshop.

Bouncing Balloon Bunny Rabbit

(BEGINNER'S LEVEL)

This adorable balloon rabbit is a variation of the balloon dog. The same twists are used, but a couple of the dimensions are different, and in order to make it sit up you'll employ a well-known balloon-sculpting technique. Don't worry; it's easy. And, if the sculpting is done correctly, the rabbit will actually sit up by itself.

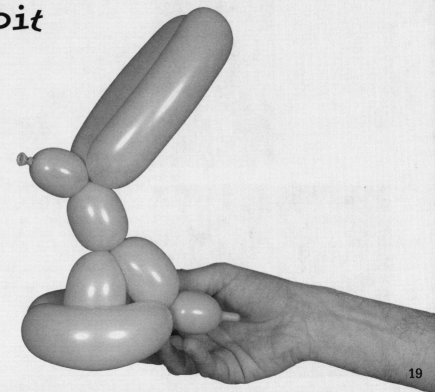

1. Pass out an inflated balloon with a four-inch tail of uninflated balloon at the end to each person who would like to participate.

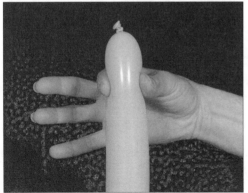

2. Ask everyone to find the end of the balloon that has the knot in it and hold the knot end of the balloon up in front of them. Everyone will begin twisting the balloon from the end that has the knot toward the end that has the tail. This will allow the air in the balloon to move downward toward the tail as you make your twists. Ask everyone to pinch the balloon with their thumb and index finger of one hand, about one inch from the knot. Demonstrate for everyone first.

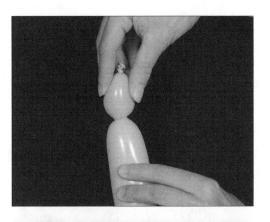

3. Ask everyone to take their free hand and twist the one-inch section of balloon around, two full turns, away from their body. This twist forms the nose of their rabbit. Be sure to demonstrate this for everyone before they try it on their own balloon.

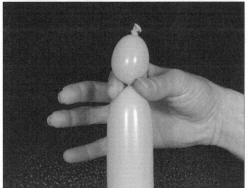

4. Tell everyone that they must hold onto this twist gently with the thumb and index finger of one hand to prevent it from untwisting. Demonstrate.

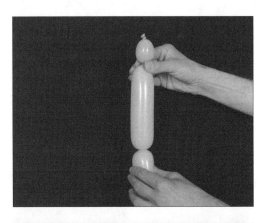

5. Ask everyone to hold onto their first twist so that it doesn't untwist and pinch their balloon six inches below that first one-inch bubble. Ask them to twist both their hands in opposite directions until their balloon twists again at the point that they are pinching. This second bubble will form one of the ears of the balloon rabbit. Again, demonstrate this move for everyone before they try it themselves.

6. Tell everyone that they must continue holding onto both twists so that they don't untwist. Demonstrate.

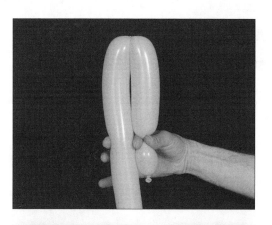

7. Ask everyone to fold the two bubbles that they have just created down alongside the length of the balloon. Show everyone how to pinch their length of balloon at the point where it meets their first twist. This will form the second ear of their rabbit. Demonstrate.

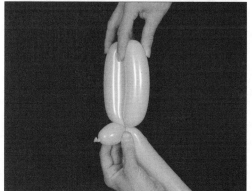

8. Ask everyone to watch this next move closely, before they try it on their own balloon. Twist both of the ears by rotating them together, about two full turns around. Demonstrate slowly, and untwist and repeat this move if people ask to see it again.

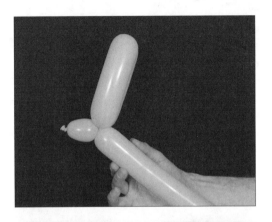

9. This third twist will lock the first two twists of everyone's animals so that everyone can let go of the nose-and-ears section of their rabbit. This twist is referred to as a *locking twist*. Everyone's hands are now free to finish the rest of their rabbits. Have everyone hold up their nose-and-ears section at this point so they can look around at each other's creations.

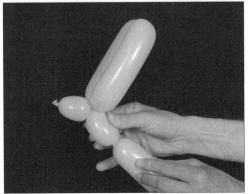

10. With everyone's nose-and-ears section of their rabbit finished and locked into place with a locking twist, have everyone pinch their balloon, with their thumb and index finger of one hand, about two inches below their nose-and-ears section. Holding one hand above and one hand below this point on their balloon, have everyone turn both their hands in opposite directions until their balloon twists at that point. This bubble will be the neck of their balloon rabbit.

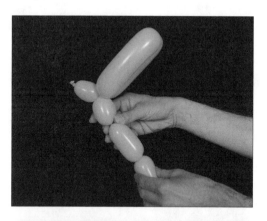

11. Show everyone again how to hold this twist gently with the thumb and index finger of one of their hands. While everyone's holding onto that twist, have them measure a three-inch bubble directly below that twist. Have them turn both their hands in opposite directions above and below this point, until the balloon twists again (at least two full turns). Remember to tell everyone that they have to hold onto both of these twists for just a couple more minutes until they make a locking twist. This second bubble will be one of their rabbit's front legs.

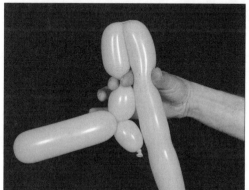

12. Have everyone fold these two bubbles down alongside their remaining length of balloon. Have them pinch their remaining length of balloon at the point where it meets the first twist. The two bubbles formed by their pinch will be the two front legs of their rabbit.

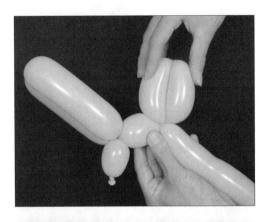

13. Have everyone twist both of the front legs around, using a locking twist, two full turns. This will lock all three of their twists and will free their hands to finish the rest of their rabbit. Everyone now has the nose, ears, neck, and front legs of their rabbit.

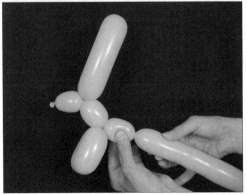

14. Have everyone pinch off another two-inch bubble beneath the neck-and-front-legs section of their rabbit. Have them go ahead and twist the balloon again at this point; by now they're pretty familiar with that move. Make sure everyone remembers to hold onto the twist gently to prevent it from untwisting. This will be the body section of everyone's rabbit.

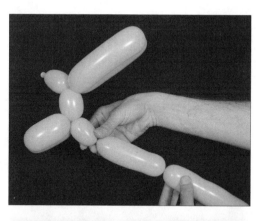

15. While everyone is gently holding that twist, have them all pinch off a four-inch bubble beneath the one that they have just made. Have them all make a twist in the balloon at this point. This second bubble will form one of their rabbit's back legs. Make sure everyone remembers to keep holding onto both twists.

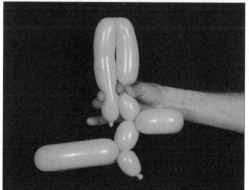

16. Have everyone fold these two bubbles down alongside the remaining length of balloon. Then have everyone pinch the last length of the balloon at the point where it meets the first twist. This bubble will form the other back leg of everyone's rabbit.

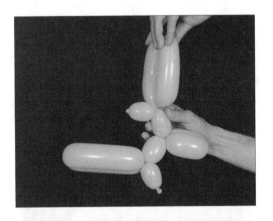

17. Have everyone use a locking twist and twist both of the back legs around two full turns. This locks the body-and-back-legs section. Be sure that everyone leaves a little bubble at the very end for their rabbit's tail.

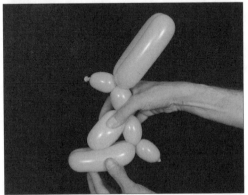

18. This next step is especially important to demonstrate for everyone *before* they try it on their own balloon. To get everyone's rabbit to sit up, have everyone push their rabbit's front legs down in between the rabbit's back legs.

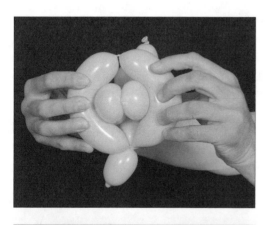

19. Have everyone gently spread the back legs of their rabbits apart and roll them around the front legs. Warn everyone not to force the front legs into the back legs but to gently *roll* the back legs around the front ones.

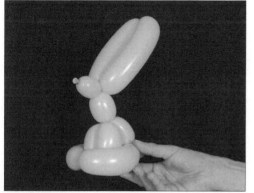

20. Congratulations! You've completed the fabulous bouncing balloon bunny rabbit. Have everyone hold their rabbit up and look around at all the different variations of rabbits that people have made.

Court Jester's Crown

(BEGINNER'S LEVEL)

Balloon hats are incredibly festive to wear and an excellent and colorful way to dress up any balloon party. Your imagination is the limit when it comes to balloon hats; you can spontaneously invent a balloon hat of your own design by twisting several balloons onto this hat using the techniques you've already mastered. Check out one of my other books, *Balloon Hats & Accessories* (Contemporary Books, 1989), for creative ideas for other ways to incorporate balloons into your wardrobe.

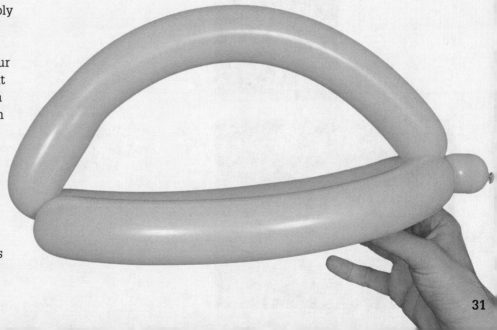

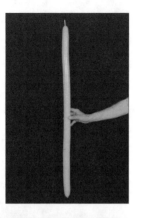

1. Pass out an inflated balloon with a one-inch tail on the end to each participant. Have each person squeeze their balloon gently, below the knot, to release some tension in the balloon.

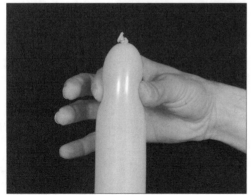

2. Have everyone locate the knot end of their balloon. Have everyone pinch their balloon, with the thumb and index finger of one hand, one inch below the knot.

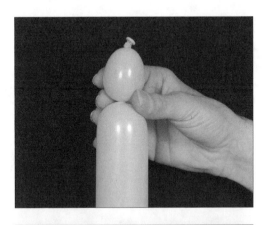

3. Have everyone twist their balloon at this point, which will form a one-inch bubble. Make sure everyone holds on to their one-inch bubble so that it doesn't untwist.

4. Have everyone wrap their balloon around the head of the person that they're making it for (it could be their own head), and have them mark with their finger where the twist meets the balloon.

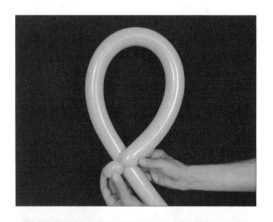

5. Have everyone take their balloon off of whoever's head that they've measured, and have them join their one-inch bubble with their length of balloon at the point that they've been marking with their finger.

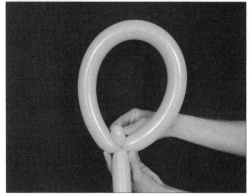

6. Have everyone twist their one-inch bubble all the way around their length of balloon at that point, until it locks. Demonstrate this step yourself before everyone tries it on their own balloon.

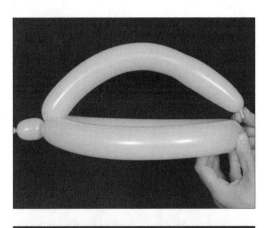

7. Have everyone hold the tail end of their balloon, and have them pull the tail over to the opposite side of the hat, creating an arc.

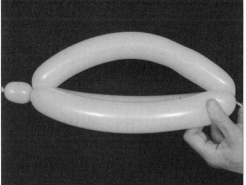

8. Show everyone how to wrap the tail of their balloon around the body of their balloon two full times, until it locks in place.

9. Tell everyone that a balloon hat doesn't actually *become* a balloon hat until somebody puts it on their head. Have everyone don their balloon hats, then pass them around and try others on.

Amazing Inflatable Balloon Giraffe

(BEGINNER'S LEVEL)

The giraffe is basically the same as the dog, but it has a much longer neck. You'll make the same twists as you did for the dog, but you'll make the neck longer and all of the other body parts slightly smaller. It's a subtle variation, but the resulting giraffe is one of the most popular balloon animals of all time.

1. Pass out an inflated balloon with a three-inch tail of uninflated balloon to each person who would like to participate.

2. Ask everyone to find the end of the balloon that has the knot in it and hold the knot end of the balloon up in front of them. You will begin twisting the balloon from the end that has the knot toward the end that has the tail. This will allow the air in the balloon to move downward toward the tail as you make your twists. Ask everyone to pinch the balloon, with the thumb and index finger of one hand, about two inches from the knot. Demonstrate for everyone first.

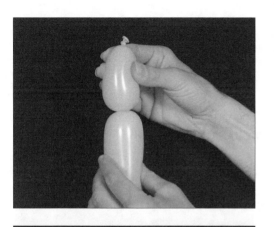

3. Ask everyone to take their free hand and twist this two-inch section of balloon around, two full turns, away from their body. This twist forms the nose of the giraffe. Demonstrate this for everyone before they try it on their own balloon.

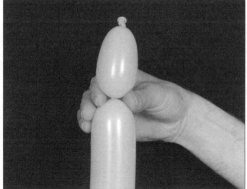

4. Tell everyone that they must hold onto this twist gently with the thumb and index finger of one hand to prevent it from untwisting. Demonstrate.

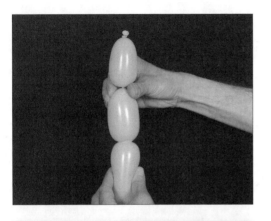

5. Ask everyone to hold onto their first twist so that it doesn't untwist and to pinch their balloon two inches below that first two-inch bubble. Ask them to twist both their hands in opposite directions until their balloon twists again at the point that they are pinching. This second bubble will form one of the ears of their balloon giraffe. Again, demonstrate this move for everyone before they try it themselves.

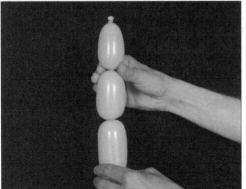

6. Tell everyone that they must continue holding onto both twists so that they don't untwist. Demonstrate.

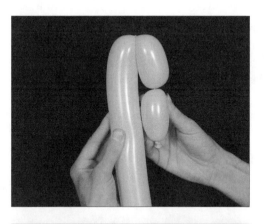

7. Ask everyone to fold the two bubbles that they have just created down alongside the length of the balloon. Demonstrate.

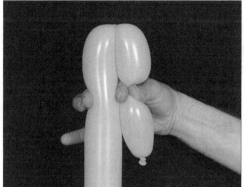

8. Show everyone how to pinch their length of balloon at the point where it meets their first twist. This pinch will form the second ear of their giraffe.

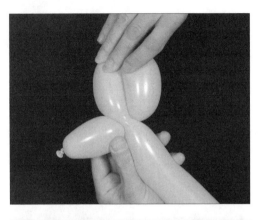

9. Ask everyone to watch this next move closely, before they try it on their own balloon. Twist both of the ears by rotating them together, about two full turns around. Demonstrate slowly, and untwist and repeat this move if people ask to see it again.

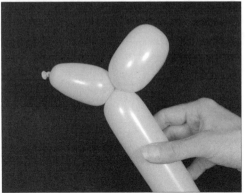

10. This third twist will lock the first two twists of everyone's animal and will allow everyone to let go of the nose-and-ears section of their giraffe. This twist is referred to as a *locking twist*. Everyone's hands are now free to finish making the rest of their giraffe. These three twists that you've just learned in making your balloon giraffe are the only three twists that you need to know to complete the giraffe. Everyone will now repeat these three twists, in their entirety, two more times, and their balloon giraffe will be finished. Have everyone hold up their nose-and-ears section at this point so everyone can look around at each other's creations.

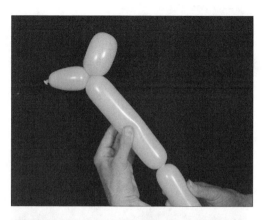

11. With everyone's nose-and-ears section of their giraffes finished and locked into place with a locking twist, have everyone pinch their balloon with their thumb and index finger of one hand about eight inches below their nose-and-ears section. (This large eight-inch bubble is for the giraffe's neck.) Holding one hand above and one hand below this point on their balloon, have everyone turn both their hands in opposite directions until their balloon twists at that point.

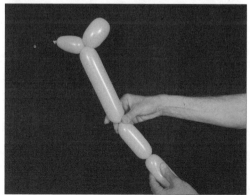

12. Show everyone again how to hold this twist gently with the thumb and index finger of one of their hands. While everyone's holding that twist, have them measure another three inches below that twist, just as they did before. Have them turn both their hands in opposite directions above and below this point, until the balloon twists again (at least two full turns). Tell everyone that they have to hold onto both of these twists for just a couple more minutes until they make a locking twist. This second bubble will be one of their giraffe's front legs.

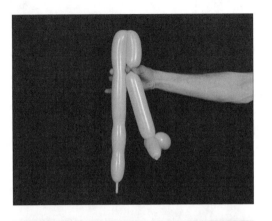

13. Have everyone fold these two bubbles down alongside their remaining length of balloon. Have them pinch their remaining length of balloon at the point where it meets the first twist. The two bubbles formed by their pinch will be the two front legs of their giraffe.

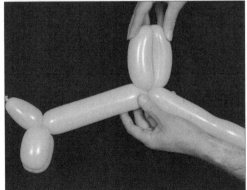

14. Have everyone twist both of the front legs around, using a locking twist, two full turns. This will lock all three of their twists and will free their hands to finish the rest of their giraffe.

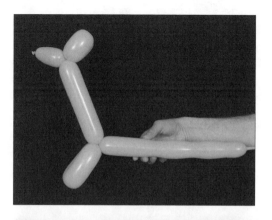

15. Everyone now has the nose, ears, neck, and front legs of their giraffe.

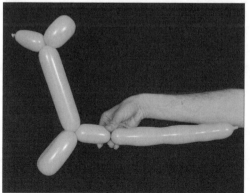

16. Have everyone pinch off a two-inch bubble beneath the neck-and-front-legs section of their giraffe. Have them go ahead and twist the balloon again at this point; by now they're pretty familiar with that move. Make sure everyone remembers to hold onto the twist gently to prevent it from untwisting. This will be the body section of everyone's giraffe.

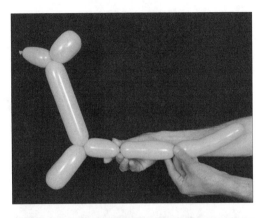

17. While everyone is gently holding that twist, have them all pinch off a three-inch bubble beneath the one that they have just made. Have them all make a twist in the balloon at this point. This second bubble will form one of their giraffe's back legs. Make sure everyone remembers to keep holding onto both twists.

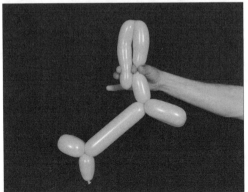

18. Have everyone fold these two bubbles down alongside the remaining length of balloon. Then have everyone pinch the last length of the balloon at the point where it meets their first twist. This bubble will form the other back leg of everyone's giraffe.

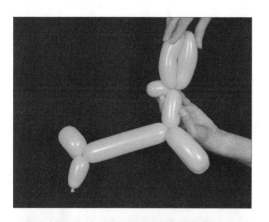

19. Have everyone use a locking twist and twist both of the back legs around two full turns. This locks the body-and-back-legs section. Be sure that everyone leaves a little bubble at the very end for their giraffe's tail.

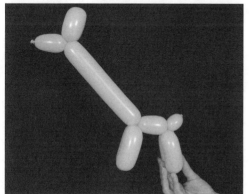

20. Have everyone play with the different parts of their balloon giraffe (gently) until it looks somewhat like the giraffe in the photo. Remember, a little variation makes for some interesting giraffes. Everyone's giraffe should look a little different. That's what gives them character and makes this a unique experience. Have everyone hold their balloon giraffe up so that each person can see all the different kinds of giraffes that everyone made. Nice going! Now, wasn't that satisfying? You just taught everyone how to make a pretty cool balloon giraffe.

Croc o' Gator: The Balloon Alligator/Crocodile

(BEGINNER'S LEVEL)

Over the years, I've gotten a million requests to create a balloon alligator or crocodile. Because I never really knew the difference between the two, this one will serve as either. Hereinafter, for purposes of clarity, this friendly balloon critter will be referred to simply as the "croc o' gator." This one is particularly fun to take home and play with after the party because it will actually float in your bathtub.

1. Pass out an inflated balloon, leaving a four-inch tail of uninflated balloon on the end, to each person who would like to participate.

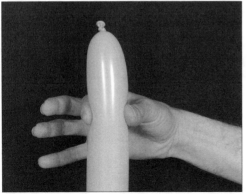

2. Ask everyone to find the end of the balloon that has the knot in it and hold the knot end of the balloon up in front of them. You will begin twisting the balloon from the end that has the knot toward the end that has the tail. This will allow the air in the balloon to move downward toward the tail as you make your twists. Ask everyone to pinch the balloon with their thumb and index finger of one hand, about three inches from the knot. Demonstrate for everyone first.

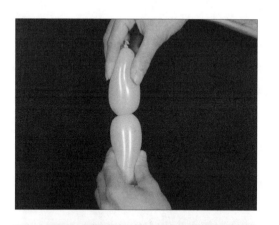

3. Ask everyone to take their free hand and twist this three-inch section of balloon around, two full turns, away from their body. This twist forms the snout of their croc o' gator. Demonstrate this for everyone before they try it on their own balloon.

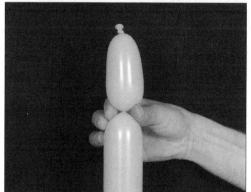

4. Tell everyone that they must hold onto this twist gently with the thumb and index finger of one hand to prevent it from untwisting. Demonstrate.

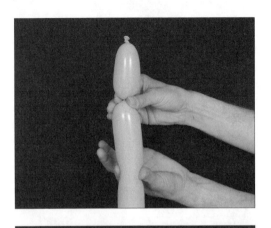

5. Ask everyone to hold onto their first twist so that it doesn't untwist and to pinch their balloon four inches below that first three-inch bubble.

6. Have everyone fold that four-inch section in half so that the pinch they are holding meets the first twist that they made.

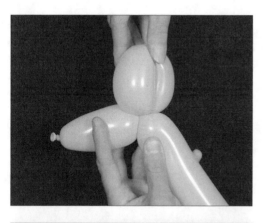

7. Have them twist the (folded) four-inch bubble around in a circle a couple of times.

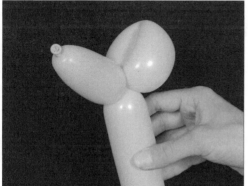

8. This will lock the folded four-inch bubble in place and will allow everyone to let go of their twists.

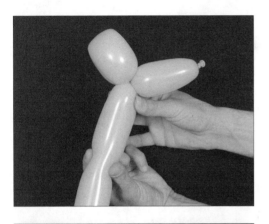

9. Everyone will now repeat that last step with another folded four-inch bubble. Have them all pinch off another four-inch bubble, directly beneath the last one.

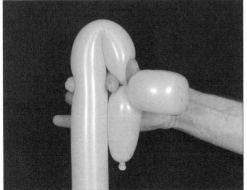

10. Have them fold their new four-inch bubble in half so that the pinch they are holding meets the same twist as before.

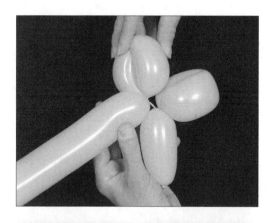

11. Have them twist the new four-inch bubble around a couple of times.

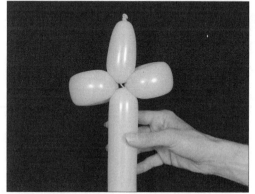

12. Hold your balloon up to show everyone what the balloon animal should look like so far. Everyone should have the snout and two front legs of their croc o' gator.

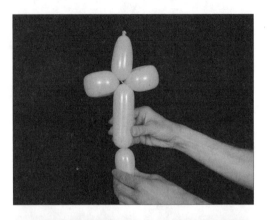

13. Have everyone pinch off and twist a five-inch bubble below the two front legs. Everyone should hold onto that twist so it doesn't untwist.

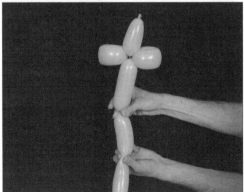

14. While everyone is holding onto that twist with one hand, have them pinch off another four-inch bubble directly beneath the five-inch bubble. Everyone will be repeating the folded four-inch bubble move that they just did twice in creating the front legs of their croc o' gator.

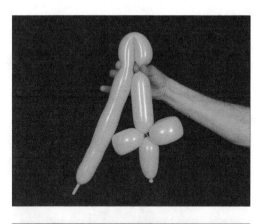

15. Show everyone again how to fold the four-inch bubble formed by their pinches in half so that the pinch they are holding meets the twist at the end of the body section.

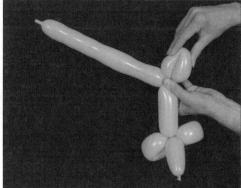

16. Have everyone twist this folded four-inch bubble around a couple of times at this point. This will lock the body section and the first of the two back legs.

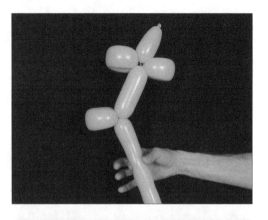

17. Everyone will now repeat that move with another folded four-inch bubble. Have everyone pinch off and twist another four-inch bubble below the first back leg.

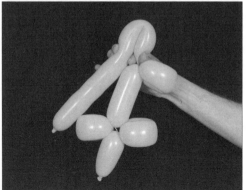

18. Have them fold their four-inch bubble in half so that the pinch they are holding meets the twist at the end of the body section.

19. Have them twist the folded four-inch bubble around a couple of times, as they have done for the other legs, to lock it in place.

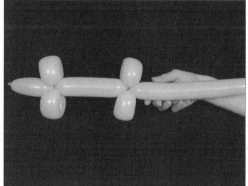

20. Hold your croc o' gator up at this point to show everyone what it should look like so far.

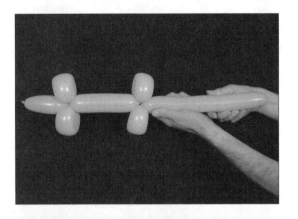

21. Have everyone *gently* squeeze the last section of their balloon, which will be the tail of their croc o' gator, so that the air expands into and fills the entire tail section.

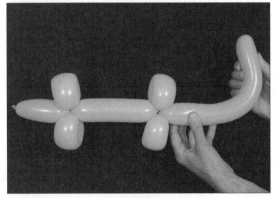

22. Have everyone gently bend the tail section with their hands to give the tail a slightly curved appearance.

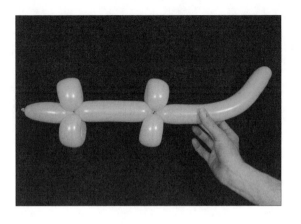

23. Nice going! You've just completed the teaching of a balloon croc o' gator. Everyone can hold their croc o' gator up and look around to see who created the fiercest looking one (it probably won't be the person using the pink balloon).

Hot Diggity Dog: The Balloon Dachshund

(BEGINNER'S LEVEL)

At some point or another, almost everyone has asked for a balloon "hot dog"—no, not the kind you eat, but the four-legged, furry kind with a tail. In fact, many people don't know that "hot dogs," those long, low, black-and-brown pooches, are actually called dachshunds. They just know that they are really cute, squat, bigheaded, unusual-looking dogs. Well, here is my balloon interpretation of that cuddly critter.

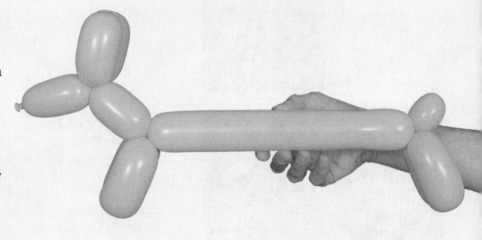

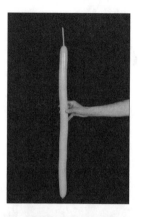

1. Pass out an inflated balloon, with a three-inch tail of uninflated balloon, to each person who would like to participate.

2. Ask everyone to find the end of the balloon that has the knot in it and hold the knot end of the balloon up in front of them. You will begin twisting the balloon from the end that has the knot toward the end that has the tail. This will allow the air in the balloon to move downward toward the tail as you make your twists. Ask everyone to pinch the balloon with their thumb and index finger of one hand, about three inches from the knot. Demonstrate for everyone first.

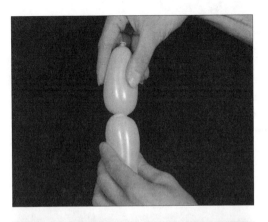

3. Ask everyone to take their free hand and twist this three-inch section of balloon around, two full turns, away from their body. This twist forms the nose of their dachshund. Demonstrate this for everyone before they try it on their own balloon.

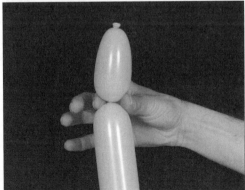

4. Tell everyone that they must hold onto this twist gently with the thumb and index finger of one hand to prevent it from untwisting. Demonstrate.

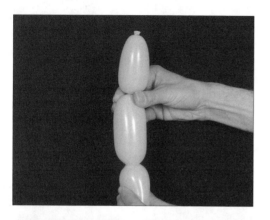

5. Ask everyone to hold onto their first twist so that it doesn't untwist and to pinch their balloon three inches below that first three-inch bubble. Ask them to twist both their hands in opposite directions until their balloon twists again at the point that they are pinching. This second bubble will form one of the ears of their balloon dachshund. Again, demonstrate this move for everyone before they try it themselves.

6. Tell everyone that they must continue holding onto both twists so that they don't untwist. Demonstrate.

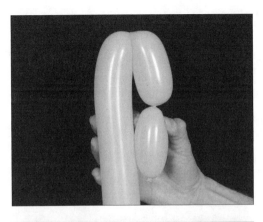

7. Ask everyone to fold the two bubbles that they have just created down alongside the length of the balloon. Demonstrate.

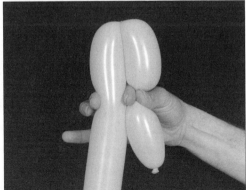

8. Show everyone how to pinch their length of balloon at the point where it meets their first twist. This will form the second ear of their dachshund.

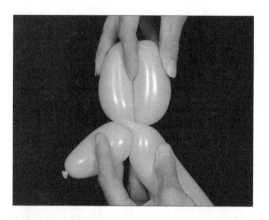

9. Ask everyone to watch this next move closely, before they try it on their own balloon. Twist both of the ears by rotating them together, about two full turns around. Demonstrate slowly, and untwist and repeat this move if people ask to see it again.

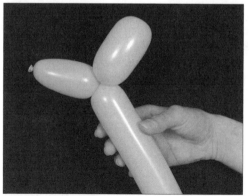

10. This third twist will lock the first two twists of everyone's animal and will allow everyone to let go of the nose-and-ears section of their dachshund. This twist is referred to as a *locking twist*. Everyone's hands are now free to finish the rest of their dachshund. The three twists that you've just demonstrated are the only three twists that you need to know to complete your balloon dachshund. Everyone will now repeat those three twists, in their entirety, two more times, and their balloon dachshund will be finished. Have everyone hold up their nose-and-ears section at this point so everyone can look around at each other's creations.

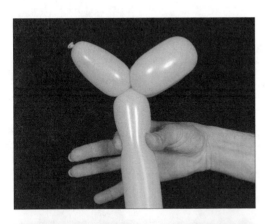

11. With everyone's nose-and-ears section of their dachshund finished and locked into place with a locking twist, have everyone pinch their balloon, with their thumb and index finger of one hand, about two inches below their nose-and-ears section.

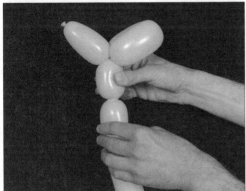

12. Holding one hand above and one hand below this point on their balloon, have everyone turn both their hands in opposite directions until their balloon twists at that point. This bubble will be the neck of their dachshund.

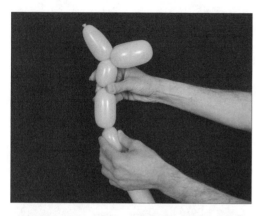

13. Show everyone again how to hold this twist gently with the thumb and index finger of one of their hands. While everyone's holding that twist, have them measure another three inches below that twist, just as they did before. Have them turn both their hands in opposite directions above and below this point, until the balloon twists again (at least two full turns). Remember to tell everyone that they have to hold onto both of these twists for just a couple more minutes until they make a locking twist. This second bubble will be one of their dachshund's front legs.

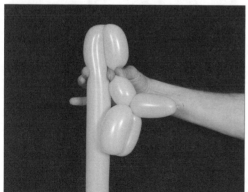

14. Have everyone fold these two bubbles down alongside their remaining length of balloon. Have them pinch their remaining length of balloon at the point where it meets the first twist. The two bubbles formed by their pinch will be the two front legs of their dachshund.

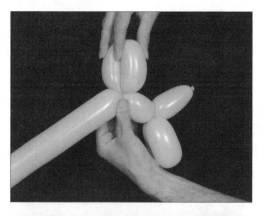

15. Have everyone twist both of the front legs around, using a locking twist, two full turns. This will lock all three of their twists and will free their hands to finish the rest of their dachshund. Everyone now has the nose, ears, neck, and front legs of their dachshund.

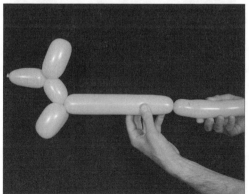

16. Have everyone pinch off a longer eight-inch bubble beneath the neck-and-front-legs section of their dachshund. Have them go ahead and twist the balloon again at this point; by now they're pretty familiar with that move. Make sure everyone remembers to hold onto the twist gently to prevent it from untwisting. This will be the body section of their dachshund.

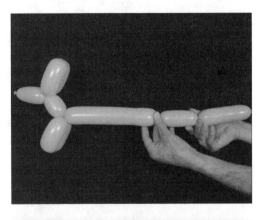

17. While everyone is gently holding that twist, have them pinch off a three-inch bubble beneath the eight-inch bubble that they have just made. Have them all make a twist in the balloon at this point. This second bubble will form one of their dachshund's back legs. Make sure everyone remembers to keep holding onto both twists.

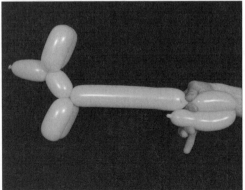

18. Have everyone fold these two bubbles down alongside the remaining length of balloon. Then have everyone pinch the last length of the balloon at the point where it meets their first twist. This bubble will form the other back leg of everyone's dachshund.

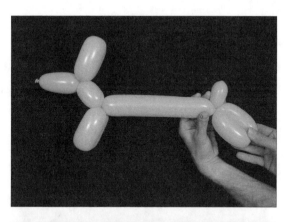

19. Have everyone use a locking twist and twist both of the back legs around two full turns. This locks the body-and-back-legs section. Be sure that everyone leaves a little bubble at the very end for their dachshund's tail.

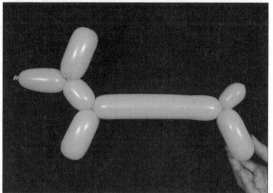

20. Have everyone play with the different parts of their balloon dachshund (gently) until it looks somewhat like the dachshund in the photo. Don't worry if your proportions are a little off; everyone will get better with practice. Have everyone hold their balloon dachshund up so that each person can see all the different kinds of dachshunds that are possible. Some have longer bodies than others. Some have bigger heads than others. Don't worry. Practice, practice, practice.

Rudolph's Cousin Murray: The Balloon Reindeer (or Moose)

(BEGINNER'S LEVEL)

What a great deal: you get two animals for the price of one, with just a single extra twist! This is another variation of the classic balloon dog. The main differences between our pal Murray and the balloon dog are the twists used in making the head of the reindeer/moose (hereinafter referred to as Murray). This balloon reindeer/moose is another excellent choice for complete beginners. Have a blast!

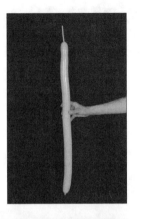

1. Pass out an inflated balloon, with a four-inch tail of uninflated balloon, to each person who would like to participate.

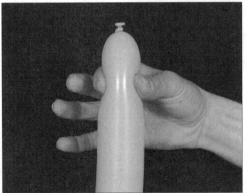

2. Ask everyone to find the end of the balloon that has the knot in it, and ask them to hold the knot end of the balloon up in front of them. You will begin twisting the balloon from the end that has the knot and twist toward the end that has the tail. This will allow the air in the balloon to move downward toward the tail as you make your twists. Ask everyone to pinch the balloon with their thumb and index finger of one hand, about one inch from the knot. Demonstrate this for everyone first.

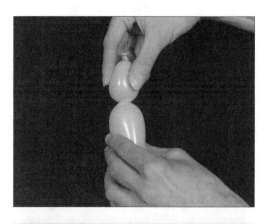

3. Ask everyone to take their free hand and twist this one-inch section of balloon around, two full turns, away from their body. This twist forms Murray's nose. Demonstrate this for everyone before they try it on their own balloon.

4. Tell everyone that they must hold onto this twist gently with the thumb and index finger of one hand to prevent it from untwisting. Demonstrate.

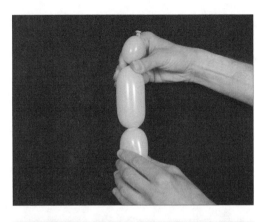

5. Ask everyone to hold onto their first twist so that it doesn't untwist and to pinch their balloon three inches below that first one-inch bubble. Ask them to twist both their hands in opposite directions until their balloon twists again at the point that they are pinching. This second bubble will form one of Murray's antlers. Again, demonstrate this move for everyone before they try it themselves.

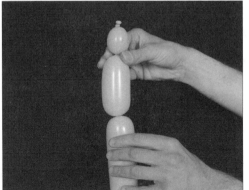

6. Tell everyone that they must continue holding onto both twists so that they don't untwist. Demonstrate.

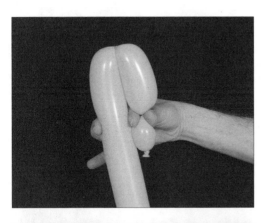

7. Ask everyone to fold the two bubbles that they have just created down alongside the length of the balloon. Demonstrate. Show everyone how to pinch their length of balloon at the point where it meets their first twist. This will form the rest of the first antler.

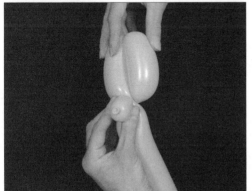

8. Ask everyone to watch this next move closely, before they try it on their own balloon. Twist both of the three-inch bubbles by rotating them together, about two full turns around. Demonstrate slowly, and untwist and repeat this move if people ask to see it again.

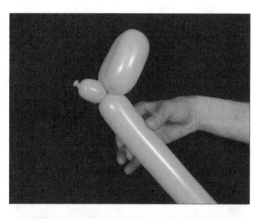

9. This third twist will lock the first two twists of everyone's animal and will allow everyone to let go of the first of Murray's antlers. This twist is referred to as a *locking twist*. Everyone's hands are now free to finish making the rest of Murray's body.

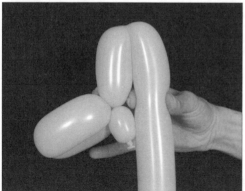

10. Everyone will now repeat the last two steps to make Murray's second antler. Have everyone make a three-inch bubble directly beneath the first antler and then fold the length of balloon down alongside this three-inch bubble.

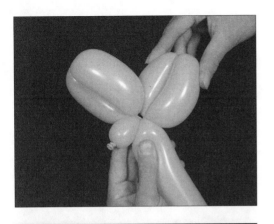

11. Have everyone measure another three-inch bubble along the length of balloon, to match the last one that they made. Have everyone join these two bubbles with a locking twist at their bases, to form a second antler.

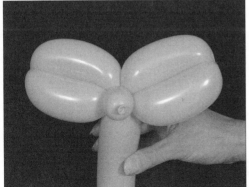

12. This is what Murray's head looks like so far. Show yours around so everyone can see.

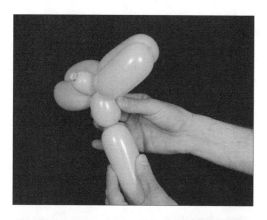

13. Instruct everyone to pinch off another two-inch bubble for the neck, directly beneath Murray's head. Have them twist the balloon at this point; they have done that move several times already.

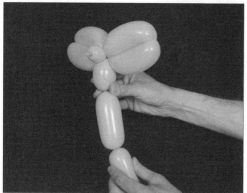

14. While everyone is gently holding that twist, have them pinch off and twist a four-inch bubble directly beneath the two-inch bubble. This four-inch bubble will be one of Murray's front legs. Make sure everyone remembers to keep holding onto both twists.

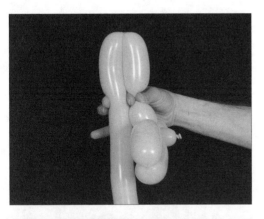

15. Have everyone fold these two bubbles down alongside the remaining length of balloon. Then have everyone pinch the remaining length of the balloon at the point where it meets their first twist. The bubble formed by their pinch will be Murray's other front leg.

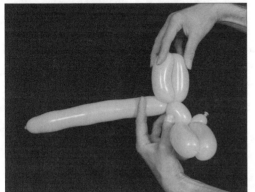

16. Have everyone use a locking twist and twist both of the front legs around in a circle, two full turns. This will lock everyone's neck-and-front-legs section and will free their hands to finish making Murray the reindeer.

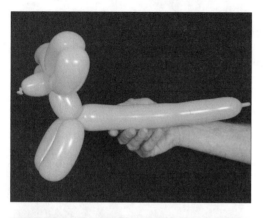

17. This is what Murray's head, neck, and front legs should look like so far.

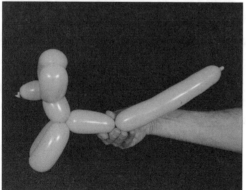

18. Now that everyone has made a few twists in their balloon, we can step up the pace a little bit. Have everyone pinch off and twist a three-inch bubble for the body. Remember to tell everyone that they must hold onto that twist gently so that it doesn't untwist.

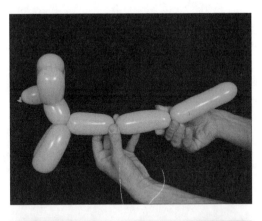

19. While everyone is gently holding onto their first twist, have them all pinch off and twist a four-inch bubble for one of Murray's back legs. Remember to tell everyone that they must continue holding onto both twists so that they don't untwist.

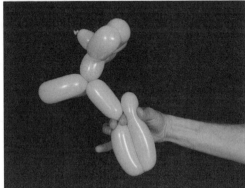

20. Have them all fold these two bubbles down alongside the remaining length of their balloon, and have them pinch the balloon where the length of balloon meets their first twist. The bubble formed by their pinch will be the second back leg.

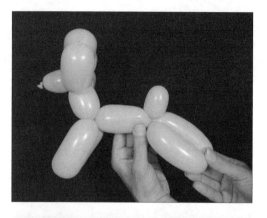

21. Have them all twist both back legs by rotating them around in a circle two full turns. Demonstrate this move for everyone before they try it on their own balloon. Untwist and repeat this move if people need to see it again.

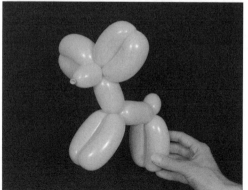

22. This last locking twist will lock Murray's body and back legs in place and will free everyone's hands. Have everyone adjust their reindeer's antlers (gently) so that they face forward, as in the picture. This is what Murray the balloon reindeer looks like. Very nice work everyone!

23. To transform Murray into a balloon moose, have everyone simply twist their reindeer's antlers forward approximately one-quarter turn, until they pop up and form a V, as in the picture. It's a simple twist, yet a totally different, new animal! The choice is yours, and you can change it back and forth as often as you'd like . . . until the balloon accidentally pops. Congratulations on the teaching of a wonderful balloon reindeer/moose. Have everyone hold their creations up to compare creatures.

Itty-Bitty Balloon Mouse

(INTERMEDIATE LEVEL)

This animal is best for people who have already had at least one previous experience making balloon animals, and younger children might have a trickier time with the smaller bubbles required for this animal.

The mouse is remarkably similar to the dog. In fact, the procedure is exactly the same, but all of the bubbles used in making the mouse are small (one-inch) bubbles, and you begin by inflating the balloon just eight inches.

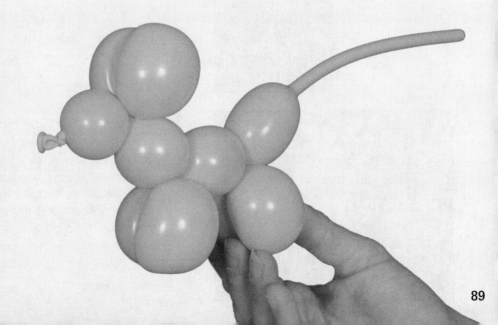

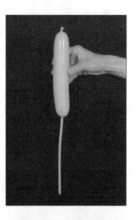

1. Pass out an inflated balloon with just eight inches of *air* (not tail) to each participant.

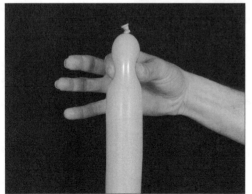

2. Ask everyone to find the end of the balloon that has the knot in it and hold the knot end of the balloon up in front of them. You will begin twisting the balloon from the end that has the knot toward the end that has the long tail. This will allow the air in the balloon to move downward toward the tail as you make your twists. Ask everyone to pinch the balloon with their thumb and index finger of one hand, one inch from the knot. Demonstrate this for everyone.

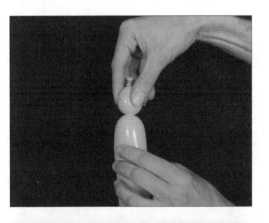

3. Ask everyone to take their free hand and twist the one-inch section of balloon around, two full turns, away from their body. This twist forms the nose of the mouse. Demonstrate this for everyone before they try it on their own balloon.

4. Tell everyone that they must hold onto this twist gently with the thumb and index finger of one hand to prevent it from untwisting. Demonstrate.

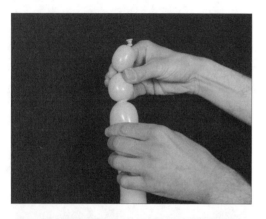

5. Ask everyone to hold onto their first twist so that it doesn't untwist and to pinch their balloon one inch below that first one-inch bubble. Ask them to twist both their hands in opposite directions until their balloon twists again at the point that they are pinching. This second bubble will form one of the ears of the balloon mouse. Again, demonstrate this move for everyone before they try it themselves.

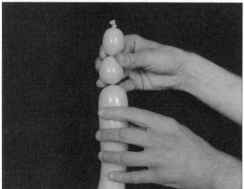

6. Tell everyone that they must continue holding onto both twists so that they don't untwist. Demonstrate.

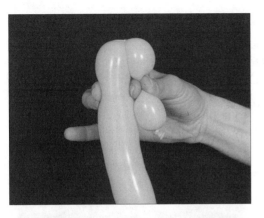

7. Ask everyone to fold the two bubbles that they have just made down alongside the length of the balloon. Demonstrate. Show everyone how to pinch their length of balloon at the point where it meets their first twist. This will form the second ear of their mouse.

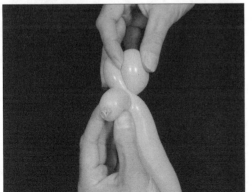

8. Ask everyone to watch this next move closely, before they try it on their own balloon. Twist both of the ears by rotating them together, about two full turns around. Demonstrate slowly, and untwist and repeat this move if people ask to see it again.

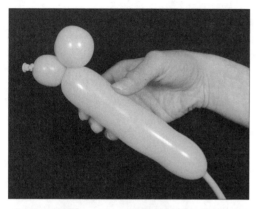

9. This third twist will lock the first two twists of everyone's animal and will allow everyone to let go of the nose-and-ears section of their mouse. This twist is referred to as a *locking twist*. Everyone's hands are now free to finish the rest of their mouse. The three twists that you've just demonstrated are the only three twists that you need to know to complete your balloon mouse. Everyone will now repeat those three twists, in their entirety, two more times, and their balloon mouse will be finished. Have everyone hold up their nose-and-ears section at this point so everyone can look around at each other's creations.

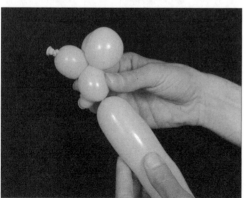

10. With everyone's nose-and-ears section of their mice finished and locked into place with a locking twist, have everyone pinch their balloon, with their thumb and index finger of one hand, about one inch below their nose-and-ears section. Holding one hand above and one hand below this point on their balloon, have everyone turn both their hands in opposite directions until their balloon twists at that point. This bubble will be the neck of their balloon mouse.

11. Show everyone again how to hold this twist gently with the thumb and index finger of one of their hands. While everyone's holding that twist, have them measure another one inch below that twist, just as they did before. Have them turn both their hands in opposite directions above and below this point, until the balloon twists again (at least two full turns). This will create a second one-inch bubble directly beneath everyone's first one-inch bubble. Remember to tell everyone that they have to hold onto both of these twists for just a couple more minutes until they make a locking twist. This second bubble will be one of their mouse's front legs.

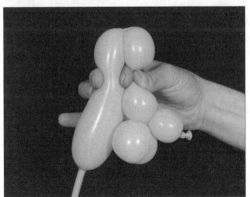

12. Have everyone fold these two one-inch bubbles down alongside their remaining length of balloon. Have them pinch their remaining length of balloon at the point where it meets the first twist. The two bubbles formed by their pinches will be the two front legs of their mouse.

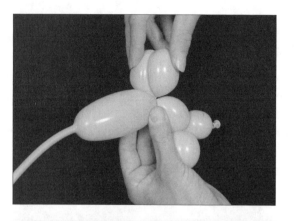

13. Have everyone twist both of the front legs around, using a locking twist, two full turns. This will lock all three of their twists and will free their hands to finish the rest of their mouse. Everyone now has the nose, ears, neck, and front legs of their mouse.

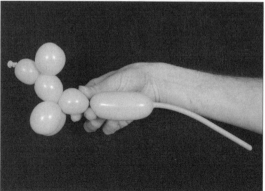

14. Have everyone pinch off another one-inch bubble beneath the neck-and-front-legs section of their mouse. Have them go ahead and twist the balloon again at this point; by now they're pretty familiar with that move. Make sure everyone remembers to hold onto the twist gently to prevent it from untwisting. This will be the body section of the mouse.

15. While everyone is gently holding onto that twist, have them pinch off another one-inch bubble beneath the one that they have just made. Have them all make a twist in the balloon at this point. This second bubble will form one of their mouse's back legs. Make sure everyone remembers to keep holding onto both twists.

16. Have everyone fold these two bubbles down alongside the remaining length of balloon. Then have everyone pinch the last length of the balloon at the point where it meets their first twist. This bubble will form the other back leg of the mouse. Be sure to leave a small bubble for the beginning of the tail. This also helps to lock the last bubbles because they are so small.

17. Have everyone use a locking twist and twist both of the back legs around two full turns. This locks the body-and-back-legs section.

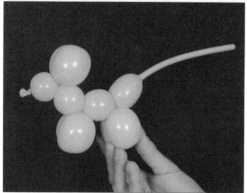

18. Have everyone play with the different parts of their balloon mouse (gently) until it looks somewhat like the mouse in the photo. Don't worry if your proportions are a little off; everyone will get better with practice. Have everyone hold their balloon mouse up so that each person can see all the different kinds of mice that everyone made. Congratulations! You've just completed the teaching of a balloon mouse (and, I trust, made a pretty cute balloon mouse yourself).

World's Smallest Balloon Elephant

(INTERMEDIATE LEVEL)

The balloon elephant is always a tremendous crowd-pleaser! The body of this animal is basically the same as that of a balloon dog, but the head, with the floppy ears and long trunk, makes him truly unique. What kind of elephant will you create: one with the trunk up or trunk down?

1. Pass out an inflated balloon, with a five-inch tail of uninflated balloon, to each person who would like to participate.

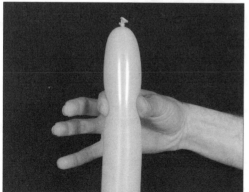

2. Ask everyone to find the end of the balloon that has the knot in it, and ask them to hold the knot end of the balloon up in front of them. You will begin twisting the balloon from the end that has the knot and twist toward the end that has the tail. This will allow the air in the balloon to move downward toward the tail as you make your twists. Ask everyone to pinch the balloon with their thumb and index finger of one hand, about three inches from the knot. Demonstrate for everyone first.

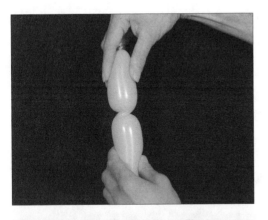

3. Ask everyone to take their free hand and twist this three-inch section of balloon around, two full turns, away from their body. This twist forms the trunk of their elephant. Demonstrate this for everyone before they try it on their own balloon.

4. Tell everyone that they must hold onto this twist gently with the thumb and index finger of one hand to prevent it from untwisting. Demonstrate.

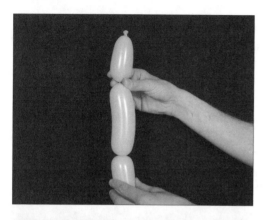

5. Ask everyone to hold onto their first twist so that it doesn't untwist. The next two bubbles, which will be the ears, are slightly different from the ears on other balloon animals. Make elephant ears by folding a six-inch bubble in half and joining it at its ends. Have everyone pinch off and twist a six-inch bubble directly beneath the three-inch bubble that they have just made.

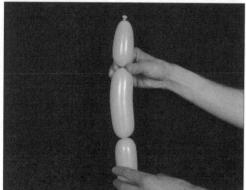

6. Make sure to tell everyone that they must continue holding onto both twists so that they don't untwist. Demonstrate.

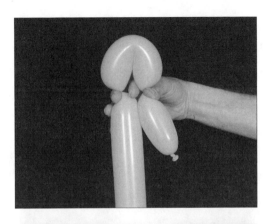

7. Have everyone fold their six-inch bubble in half, end-to-end.

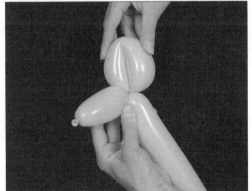

8. Have everyone twist the six-inch bubble around on its ends until it locks.

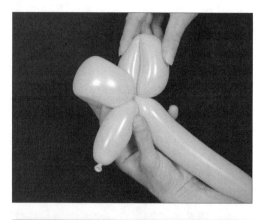

9. Everyone will now repeat this process with a second six-inch bubble, directly beneath the first folded six-inch bubble. This will be the elephant's second ear.

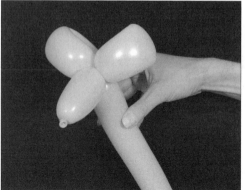

10. This is a balloon elephant's head (so far). Have everyone hold up their creation at this point so they can look around and see what everyone else made.

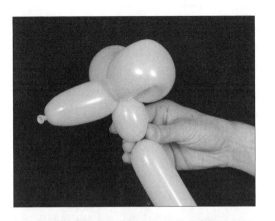

11. With everyone's elephant's head finished so far, have everyone pinch their balloon, with their thumb and index finger of one hand, about two inches beneath the head. Holding one hand above and one hand below this point on their balloon, have everyone turn both their hands in opposite directions until their balloon twists at that point. This bubble will be the neck of their elephant.

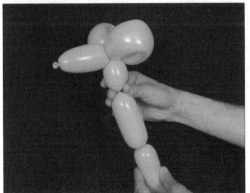

12. Show everyone again how to hold this twist gently with the thumb and index finger of one of their hands. While everyone's holding onto that twist, have them measure and pinch off a three-inch bubble directly beneath the two-inch bubble. Have them turn both their hands in opposite directions above and below this point, until the balloon twists again (at least two full turns). Remember to tell everyone that they have to hold onto both of these twists for just a couple more minutes until they make a locking twist. This second bubble will be one of their elephant's front legs.

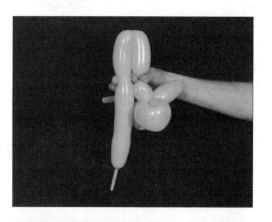

13. Have everyone fold these two bubbles down alongside their remaining length of balloon. Have them pinch their remaining length of balloon at the point where it meets the first twist. The two bubbles formed by their pinches will be the two front legs of their elephant.

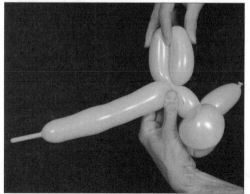

14. Have everyone twist both of the front legs around, using a locking twist, two full turns. This will lock all three of their twists and will free their hands to finish the rest of their elephant. Everyone now has the trunk, ears, neck, and front legs of their elephant.

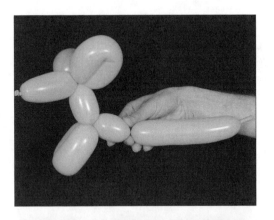

15. Have everyone pinch off another two-inch bubble beneath the neck-and-front-legs section of their elephant. Have them go ahead and twist the balloon again at this point; by now they're pretty familiar with that move. Make sure everyone remembers to hold onto the twist gently to prevent it from untwisting. This will be the body section of everyone's elephant.

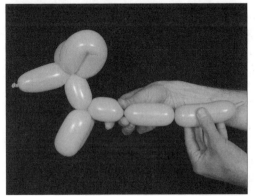

16. While everyone is gently holding that twist, have them pinch off a three-inch bubble beneath the two-inch bubble that they have just made. Have them all make a twist in the balloon at this point. This second bubble will form one of their elephant's back legs. Make sure everyone remembers to keep holding onto both twists.

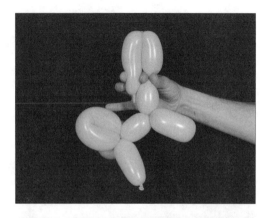

17. Have everyone fold these two bubbles down alongside the remaining length of balloon. Then have everyone pinch the last length of the balloon at the point where it meets their first twist. This bubble will form the other back leg of everyone's elephant.

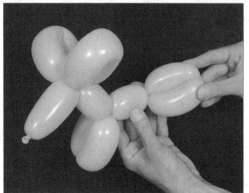

18. Have everyone use a locking twist and twist both of the back legs around two full turns. This locks the body-and-back-legs section. Be sure that everyone leaves a little bubble at the very end for their elephant's tail.

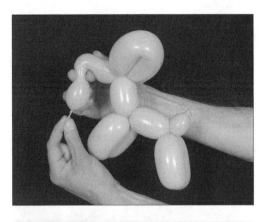

19. Have everyone bend the trunk of their elephant in half and *gently* squeeze it with one hand. At the same time have them give a gentle tug on the knot to release a little extra balloon at the knot.

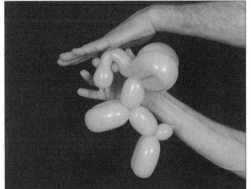

20. Have everyone rub the bend in their trunk lightly. This will give a slight curve to the elephant's trunk.

21. Now everyone has to decide the big question—trunk up, or trunk down? Have everyone decide which direction they want their elephant's trunk to point, and have them position their trunk accordingly. Congratulations! You've just taught everyone how to make one of the all-time favorite crowd-pleasers—a balloon elephant. This is what it looks like (trunk down).

Elegant Balloon Swan

(INTERMEDIATE LEVEL)

The balloon swan is one of the most graceful balloon animals you can make. Its elegant, arching neck makes it a vision to behold, but what's really cool about it is the fact that it will float in your bathtub, pool, or birdbath. Don't worry if the neck of your swan ends up being a little too short; you can always turn it into an ugly duckling.

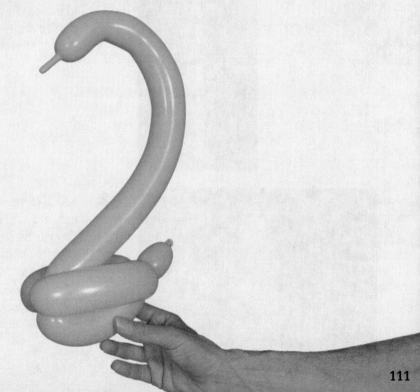

1. Pass out an inflated balloon, with a three-inch tail of uninflated balloon, to each person who would like to participate. Have everyone gently squeeze their balloon below the knot to lessen the tension.

2. Ask everyone to find the end of the balloon that has the knot in it and hold the knot end of the balloon up in front of them. You will begin twisting the balloon from the end that has the knot toward the end that has the tail. This will allow the air in the balloon to move downward toward the tail as you make your twists. Ask everyone to pinch the balloon with their thumb and index finger of one hand, about one inch from the knot. Demonstrate this for everyone.

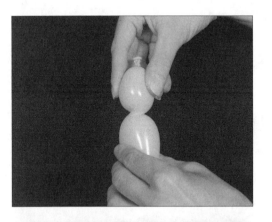

3. Ask everyone to take their free hand and twist this one-inch section of balloon around, two full turns, away from their body. The balloon swan is made backward, so this one-inch bubble will actually be the tail of the swan. Demonstrate this for everyone before they try it on their own balloon.

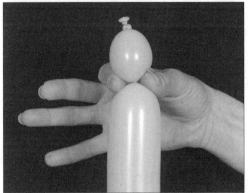

4. Tell everyone that they must hold onto this twist gently with the thumb and index finger of one hand to prevent it from untwisting. Demonstrate.

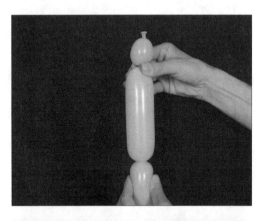

5. Ask everyone to hold onto their first twist so that it doesn't untwist and to pinch their balloon five inches below that first one-inch bubble. Ask them to twist both their hands in opposite directions until their balloon twists again at the point that they are pinching. This second bubble will form part of the body of their balloon swan. Again, demonstrate this move for everyone before they try it themselves. Tell everyone that they must continue holding onto both twists so that they don't untwist. Demonstrate.

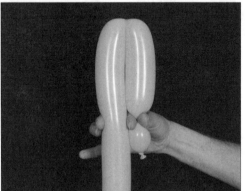

6. Ask everyone to fold the two bubbles that they have just created down alongside the length of the balloon. Have them pinch their length of balloon at the point where it meets their first twist. This will form another part of the body of their swan. Demonstrate.

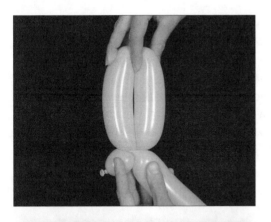

7. Ask everyone to watch this next move closely, before they try it on their own balloon. Twist both of the five-inch bubbles by rotating them together, about two full turns around. Demonstrate slowly, and untwist and repeat this move if people ask to see it again.

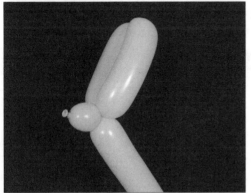

8. This third twist will lock the first two twists of everyone's animal and will allow everyone to let go of the tail-and-body section of their swan. This twist is referred to as a *locking twist*. Everyone's hands are now free to finish the rest of their swan.

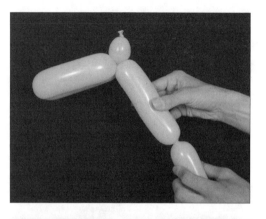

9. With everyone's tail-and-body section of their swan finished and locked into place with a locking twist, have everyone pinch their balloon, with their thumb and index finger of one hand, another five inches below their tail-and-body section. Holding one hand above and one hand below this point on their balloon, have everyone turn both their hands in opposite directions until their balloon twists at that point. This bubble will be another part of the body of their balloon swan.

10. Show everyone how to gently pull the first two five-inch bubbles apart and to push the third five-inch bubble between them.

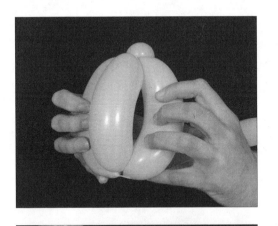

11. Show them how to gently roll the first two five-inch bubbles around the third five-inch bubble until the third bubble is all the way through the first two bubbles. Remember to tell everyone to *roll* the outer bubbles around the third five-inch bubble, not to force the third five-inch bubble through the outer ones.

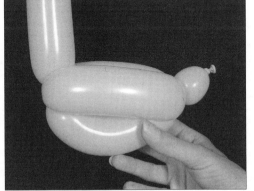

12. Have everyone hold their balloon so that two of the five-inch bubbles are on top.

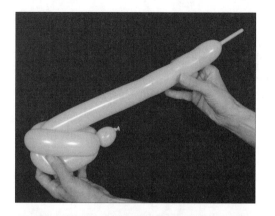

13. Show everyone how to take one hand and gently separate these two top five-inch bubbles and to pull the long length of balloon back between them.

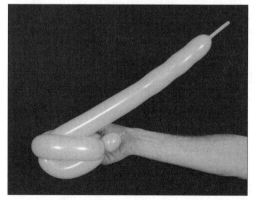

14. Have everyone press the length of their balloon snugly between the two top five-inch bubbles until it stays in place and points straight backward.

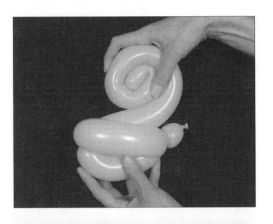

15. Have them all roll the long length of balloon (the swan's neck) up into a coil.

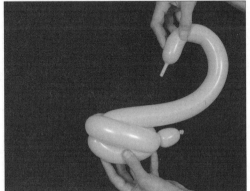

16. Have them all roll the neck of their swan back and forth until the neck is shaped just right. They can do this several times and keep playing with it until it looks the way they want it to look.

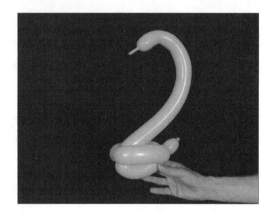

17. Congratulations! This is what a balloon swan looks like. Pass everyone's balloon swans around to compare and contrast. Remember, no two swans ever look exactly alike. Good work!

CHAPTER 2

Fun, Fantastical Balloon Party Games

Balloon party games have thrilled partygoers for decades, even centuries, and have made family and work events, birthday parties, and celebrations of every kind a little bit more lively than they might otherwise have been. Who can't remember some memorable party, family event, or extravaganza where balloons played a major role, whether it was tossing water balloons or simply having big bunches of balloons decorating the party site?

In this section, you're going to put balloons to work in 10 hilariously fun balloon games. In the following pages, you'll find instructions and rules for wonderfully interactive games that anyone can play using round balloons that they can easily buy from a local convenience, grocery, or party store. Good luck!

Blowing Hot Air: The Great Balloon and Straw Race

Objective

Blow an inflated balloon across a finish line using just a straw.

How to Play the Game

1. Designate a playing area where you can set up a starting line and a finish line approximately 10 to 20 feet apart. The surface of the playing area should be comfortable enough for people to be able to crawl on their hands and knees.
2. Designate a starting line and a finish line.
3. Inflate five different-colored round balloons and hand them out to the first five players.
4. Give each of these players a straw. You could spice things up by providing the players with multicolored straws or fun straws that have loops and twists in them, which they can take home after the party. Just make sure the straws are light enough to hold in the players' mouths using only their teeth and lips but no hands.
5. Have the five players line up at the starting line. Have them place their balloons on the ground in front of them.
6. Have each of the players put their straws in their mouths and get on their hands and knees behind their balloons.
7. Tell the players that when you give the signal they should start blowing their balloons toward the finish line as fast as possible. Tell them that they may move their balloons only by blowing through their straws. They may not touch the balloons with their hands.

8. Give the signal. The first player across the finish line is the winner of that round.

9. Pass the balloons and new straws to the remaining players and repeat the process. Have the winner of the first round engage in a playoff race with the winner of the second round. The winner of that race wins the overall race. Congratulations!

Soak City: The All-Time Classic Water-Balloon Toss

This game must be played outdoors!

Objective

Keep your water-filled balloon intact while tossing it back and forth with your partner at ever-increasing distances.

How to Play the Game

1. Be outside! Designate a large enough playing area so that five pairs will be able to eventually stand up to 20 feet away from each other, all at the same time.
2. Fill enough round balloons with water so that each pair has a water balloon. Don't overfill the balloons. Each balloon should be only six to eight inches in diameter when it is filled with water. Tie a knot in each balloon!
3. Have all participants pair off with a partner.
4. Have each of the pairs face each other, standing just one foot apart.
5. At a given signal, have each of the pairs begin tossing their balloon back and forth. After they've tossed it back and forth once, have each of the players take one step backward.

6. Then have the players toss their balloon back and forth once again.

7. Gradually, some of the balloons will begin to burst, either by someone accidentally dropping their balloon or by the balloon just breaking as it lands in a player's hands. This is a tremendous thrill and will provide a great deal of anxiety and excitement as the players attempt to preserve their balloons.

8. Continue tossing the balloons back and forth, followed by each player taking a step backward, until just one pair has a balloon still intact. That pair is the winner of the Classic Water-Balloon Toss. And they're still dry!

Blow, Tie, Burst!

Objective

Inflate, tie, and sit on a balloon until it bursts, all faster than anyone else.

How to Play the Game

1. Pass out a round balloon to each of the contestants.
2. At a given signal, each player will blow their balloon up with their mouth and then tie a knot in their balloon.
3. As soon as their knot is tied, they will each sit on their balloons until the balloons pop. They might have to bounce on their balloons a bit to get them to pop. They can pop their balloons only by sitting on

them. Using their fingers is not allowed. Remind each player before the game begins that the fuller the balloon, the easier it pops.

4. Make sure every player is holding their balloon at the same time, and give a "3, 2, 1 . . . *go*" countdown so that everyone starts at the same time.

5. The first player to blow up, tie, and burst their balloon by sitting on it wins!

Two-to-Tango: The Linked-Up Partners Balloon-Tapping Race

Objective

Tap a balloon back and forth with your partner while being the first pair to advance from a starting line across a finish line while linked at your elbows.

How to Play the Game

1. Designate a playing area, inside or out, large enough for three pairs of players to race across while batting a balloon back and forth to each other. The starting line should be *at least* 10 feet from the finish line.
2. Have all the players pick a partner.
3. Give each of the pairs an inflated round balloon.
4. Divide the pairs into two groups, and line up three of the pairs at the starting line. Have them all face the finish line.

5. Have each of the pairs link their arms together—one player's right arm linked at the elbow with the other player's left arm.

6. Have one partner in each pair hold the balloon, and have them all get ready for a starting signal.

7. When you say "go," each player holding a balloon will toss it in the air and bat it toward the free hand of their partner, while moving toward the finish line.

8. Their partner will then tap it back with their free hand. The partners must tap the balloon back and forth while moving as quickly as they can toward the finish line. Their speed will be determined by how well they're able to tap the balloon back and forth and move forward at the same time.

9. The balloons cannot hit the ground; they must stay afloat.

10. The partners' arms must remain linked at the elbows at all times. This will result in a playful tugging at each other while each partner tries to chase the balloon and tap it back.

11. When the first group of three pairs finishes, run the race again with the remaining pairs. The winners of the first group can then race against the winners of the second group.

Balloon Hockey

This game is a tremendous amount of fun and excitement and can also get extremely lively and loud. For this reason, it's best to avoid playing it in an area where there are lots of fragile, breakable items. Be sure to move all delicate items (lamps, furniture, dishware, et cetera) out of the way before you play. Be careful, but have a great time!

Objective

Your team tries to bat a balloon across the other team's goal line, while at the same time defending your own goal line.

How to Play the Game

1. Divide the players into two teams. If you have an average-size room, you should limit the teams to three or four players per team. However, the game can be played with as few as two players per team or as many as five per team.
2. Designate a playing area that is roughly rectangular in size (could be just a living room or play room), and mark off goal lines at each of the long ends of the space. You can do this with masking tape on the floor or simply by placing chairs across from each other to designate a goal line.
3. Have the teams line up, facing each other, about three feet apart from each other, in the center of the playing area.

4. Instruct the two teams that you will toss a balloon up in the air between them. Let them know that they can use any of their body parts to keep the balloon afloat but that the balloon cannot hit the ground at any time.

5. The two teams will each attempt to bat the balloon toward their own goal line while trying to prevent the other team from advancing in the opposite direction. Players may hit the balloon successively as many times as they need, as long as the balloon never touches the floor.

6. If the balloon touches the floor, play is stopped and the teams will line up again at the center of the playing area and begin again. If the balloon pops, play is also stopped and the teams will line up again with a new balloon.

7. A goal is scored each time one team advances the balloon across the other team's goal line. After each goal the teams line up again in the center of the playing area and begin again. The first team to score five goals wins that round. This game may be played through several rounds and with several different teams. If you play with several different teams, the winners of the individual rounds can eventually play each other in a playoff round.

Last One to Touch It: "Hot Potato" with a Balloon

Objective

Avoid being the one caught holding the balloon while it is batted around in a circle.

How to Play the Game

1. Inflate a round balloon.
2. Have all the players sit in a circle with about two feet between each of the players.
3. Blindfold one of the players, and have the blindfolded player sit in the middle of the circle.
4. Have one of the players in the circle hold the inflated balloon.
5. When the blindfolded player in the middle of the circle says "go," the player with the balloon will toss the balloon up in the air and tap it to the person sitting next to them.
6. That person will catch the balloon with both hands and then toss it back up in the air and tap it to the next person sitting next to them.

is in the air when the person in the middle calls "stop," the person who touched it last must leave the circle. Gradually the circle will get smaller and smaller until there is just one person left. That person is the winner of that round and gets to be the blindfolded person in the middle for the next round. This game can be played over and over again because the results are different every time and the tension and suspense are high each time.

7. This "catch-and-tap" process will continue from person to person as the balloon moves around the circle.

8. The person sitting in the middle of the circle may yell out "stop" at any time after they have said "go." (It's usually a little more fun to wait a few minutes before calling "stop," but it can occasionally be an unexpected surprise to yell "stop" quickly.) Whoever is holding the balloon when the person in the middle says "stop" will have to leave the circle. If the balloon

Under-Your-Legs and Over-Your-Heads Balloon Team Relay

Objective

Be the first team to pass a balloon to each other, first through your legs and then over your heads, back and forth through your line.

How to Play the Game

1. Divide the players into two teams of approximately five players each. (This game can be played with teams as small as four players each, but it is more exciting with large teams, if possible.)
2. Inflate a round balloon for each team.
3. Have each of the teams line up, all facing the same direction. Have the players stand approximately two feet apart from each other.
4. Hand an inflated balloon to the player at the front of each team's line.
5. At a given signal ("ready, set, *go*" works really well), the players holding the balloons bend over and pass the balloons through their legs to the players standing behind them.

6. The second players grab the balloons and pass them back through their own legs to the players standing behind them.

7. The balloons are passed this way until they reach the last players in the line.

8. When the last players grab hold of the balloons, they hold onto them with both hands and yell "turn!" At that point all of the team members turn around and face the opposite direction. The players holding the balloons then pass the balloons over their heads to the players now standing behind them.

9. These players grab the balloons with both hands and pass them back over their heads to the players standing behind them. The balloons are passed back through each line this way until they reach the last players in line (the players that started the game originally).

10. As soon as the last players are holding onto the balloons with both hands, they will yell "done!" The team that finishes the balloon-passing relay back and forth through their line, first passing the balloons through their legs and then passing them back over their heads, is the winning team. This game can be repeated and can be played with several teams if you have a large crowd. The winning teams can eventually play against each other, or the same teams can play several times against each other. Also, you can mix up the teams each time, and the results will be wildly different. Remember, the larger the team, the more crazy and wild the game will be. You can also invent your own ways of passing the balloons. For instance, you can add a round of tapping the balloons from person to person to your relay, thus prolonging the game. Each team would pass the balloons through their line, first through their legs, then back over their heads, and then once again through the line tapping it from player to player. Can you think of any other zany ways to pass the balloons through the line? Have a blast!

Balloon/Tummy Race

This is an incredibly simple yet endlessly and squealingly fun game to play with partners. Try to pick partners that are approximately the same height so that their bellies are at about the same level. They'll be holding a balloon pressed between their tummies, with no hands!

Objective

Hold a balloon between your tummy and your partner's tummy, and race from starting line to finish line faster than all the other pairs.

How to Play the Game

1. Have everyone pick a partner.

2. Designate a playing area at least 10 feet long, and mark off a starting line and a finish line.

3. Give each pair an inflated round balloon, and line up three pairs at a time at the starting line.

4. Have each of the pairs place the balloon between their bellies, and have them press their bellies together until the balloon is held in place by their bellies alone. No hands may be used to hold the balloon in place.

5. At a given signal ("ready, set, *go*") the pairs will all try to advance to the finish line any way they can, while still holding the balloon in between their tummies. This is harder than it sounds. The results are fabulous!

The first pair across the finish line with their balloon still in between their tummies is the winner.

7. Repeat the race with all the remaining pairs, and then have the winners of each round race each other. Switch the pairs around and do it again. The results are always different, and it really is harder than it seems. You'll see!

6. If a pair's balloon falls and hits the ground or if it pops, that pair must, unfortunately, leave the game.

Balloonees: The Balloon/ Knee-Press Relay

This is another tricky version of the classic balloon relay race, this time carrying the balloon in between your legs. It's more difficult than you think to move quickly (or at all) while keeping a balloon pressed between your knees.

Objective

Be the first team to have each member race from starting line to finish line while keeping a balloon pressed between their knees.

How to Play the Game

1. Designate a playing area where you can mark off a starting line and a finish line that are 10 to 20 feet apart.
2. Divide all of the players into two teams, and have each of the teams line up in single file behind the starting line.
3. Inflate one round balloon for each team, and also inflate a couple of extra balloons in case a balloon pops during the race.
4. Hand an inflated balloon to the first player in line for each team.

5. Give a starting signal ("ready, set, *go*"). At the signal, each team's first racer will place the balloon in between their legs and will proceed from the starting line to the finish line any way they can, without dropping the balloon and without using their hands. If the balloon ever falls and touches the floor, that player must pick it up and return to the starting line and begin again. If the balloon ever pops, that player must return to the starting line and get another balloon to begin again. Suggested methods of moving include walking (if you can manage!), hopping, or shuffling if all else fails.

6. When each player crosses the finish line they can grab the balloon with their hands and run it back to the next person in line.

7. That person will then place the balloon in between their knees and proceed to the finish line. This process is repeated until the entire team has finished.

8. As soon as the last player in either team has crossed the finish line, that team has won the relay race.

Balloon Stompers

This game is a loud, lively, and rambunctious balloon-popping fest! It needs to be played in an area where a large amount of squealing, laughing, and screaming can be had.

Objective

With an inflated balloon tied to your ankle with a piece of string, try to break the other players' balloons with your feet (stomping only, no kicking), while at the same time trying to protect your own balloon. Be the last player with an unbroken balloon.

How to Play the Game

1. Designate a square or rectangular playing area that will accommodate all of the players.
2. Inflate a round balloon for each player, and give each player the round balloon and a three-foot piece of string.
3. Have each player tie one end of their string around the knot of the balloon and the other end of the string around one of their ankles. The balloon should be separated from their ankle by about two feet of string.

4. Have all of the players enter the designated playing area with their balloons tied to their ankles. Give a starting signal.

5. At the starting signal, each of the players will try to break the other players' balloons using only their feet. Breaking may be done by stomping only, definitely no kicking. Any player who steps on another player's toes must leave the game.

6. Players must stay within the boundaries of the playing area. If any player leaves the playing area they must also leave the game.

7. No player may use their hands to hold other players or to pop any other balloons.

8. The best way to defend your own balloon is to use your ankle string to tug your balloon out of harm's way.

9. When a player's balloon breaks, that player must leave the playing area.
10. The last player left standing with an unbroken balloon is the winner.

A Few Funny Remarks You Can Use

When a Balloon Accidentally Pops

You say, "You've just created the most realistic-looking of all balloon animals. It's the only one that looks *exactly* like what it is—*the worm*!" (Hold up the popped, shriveled balloon.)

When Someone Asks "How Did You Learn to Do This?"

You say, "I thought this was origami!"

When Someone Asks "How Often Do They Pop?"

You say, "Just once!"

Mail-Order Sources

If you can't find sculpting balloons or a pump in your local magic, joke, or novelty shop, try one of these mail-order sources. All balloons are $18.00 a bag, postage and handling included, and come packaged 144 balloons to a bag. They are the highest-quality premium balloons available. All pumps are $6.00 each, postage and handling included. Please use U.S. currency on all orders and include an additional $5.00 postage on all orders going outside the United States.

Balloon Animals*
P.O. Box 711
Medford, MA 02155

Balloonology*
P.O. Box 301
Cambridge, MA 02238

*Massachusetts residents add 5 percent sales tax (90 cents per bag, 30 cents per pump).

About the Author

Aaron Flanders (formerly Aaron Hsu-Flanders) is the bestselling author of *Balloon Animals*, *Balloon Hats & Accessories*, *More Balloon Animals*, and *Balloon Cartoons and Other Favorites* (Contemporary Books). His books have sold more than one million copies, and he is responsible, through his books and workshops, for having taught a whole generation of clowns, magicians, and other children's performers how to sculpt balloons. Aaron's balloon prowess has been featured in *Harper's* magazine, on National Public Radio's *This American Life*, on a Cellular One radio ad, and on the QVC home-shopping network. He lives in Cambridge, Massachusetts.